The Poker-Faced Princess

The Poker-Faced Princess

Gwyneth Vacher

Illustrated by Annabel Spenceley

HODDER AND STOUGHTON
LONDON SYDNEY AUCKLAND TORONTO

To Natalie, Alys and Mij

British Library Cataloguing in Publication Data

Vacher, Gwyneth
  The poker-faced princess.
  I. Title   II. Spenceley, Annabel
  823'.914 [J]   PZ7

  ISBN 0-340-40297-0

Published by Hodder and Stoughton Children's Books,
a division of Hodder and Stoughton Ltd,
Mill Road, Dunton Green, Sevenoaks, Kent TN13 2YJ

Photoset by Rowland Phototypesetting Ltd,
Bury St Edmunds, Suffolk

Printed in Great Britain by St Edmundsbury Press Ltd,
Bury St Edmunds, Suffolk

Contents

I

No Sense of Humour

There was once a King, a very jolly King, who had almost everything in the world he wanted. Everything, that is, except a jolly daughter. The princess was satisfactory in every other way, being good to look at, with charming manners, and devoted to her parents. The only thing lacking was her ability to laugh or to smile.

'Does it matter so very much?' asked the Queen.

'Of course it does,' replied the King.

He loved to make people laugh and was constantly thinking up new ways of doing so. This often took the form of practical jokes, some of which were not always kind ones.

'Comes of having no sense of humour,' he added.

'How do you know that?' asked the Queen.

'Know what?' replied the King.

'That she has no sense of humour.'

'It's perfectly obvious. When have you ever heard her laugh? Or seen her smile for that matter? Takes after you in that respect.'

The Queen ignored this and said, 'She often used to chuckle when she was little.'

'Well, she doesn't chuckle now,' replied the King crossly.

'I really cannot understand why it should upset you so,' said the Queen. 'She seems perfectly content to me.'

'"Seems" is right,' said the King. 'You never could see any further than your nose.'

'I can see just as far as I want to see,' retorted the Queen, who was beginning to get annoyed. 'I can see the Princess now, crossing the lawn towards the pavilion. See how gracefully she moves and how her gown becomes her.'

'That's all you can think about, clothes! It's her future I'm concerned about. How is she going to find herself a husband if she goes on as she is now? No man, no self-respecting man, is going to take on a gal who has no sense of humour,' replied the King.

'She has other qualities,' said the Queen.

'I know that, and you know that, but we have had a lifetime to find out. A man sees only what is set in front of him, and would balk at having that poker-face sitting opposite him at the breakfast table every morning.'

'If this mythical man of yours can see no further than that, then he doesn't deserve my daughter,' said the Queen. 'In any case, she may not want to marry.'

'Want has nothing to do with it. Every gal needs a husband and princesses more than most,' replied the King. 'Who is going to care for her and maintain the Kingdom when we are no longer here?'

'You have a point there,' replied the Queen.

'I have ten of them,' replied the King, holding up his ten widespread fingers. 'And one more if you include this.' And here he put out his tongue tapered to a fine point. 'Ha, ha, ha.'

'Pray, don't be so disgusting,' said the Queen.

'Perhaps I was going a bit far,' conceded the King. 'Come and sit down, wife, and let us talk things over sensibly.'

Here he took his Queen's hand, and led her to a gilded couch close by an open window, where they both sat down to watch the Princess who was playing ball with her ladies.

Every now and then one or other of the ladies would shriek or laugh aloud with glee, as the ball was let fall or flew high overhead. But not the princess. Her manner remained so quiet and composed throughout the game that even the Queen was concerned.

'What is to be done, husband?' she said at length. 'There must be someone, somewhere, who can help us.'

'We will advertise, wife, that is what we will do,' replied the King.

'For a physician?' asked the Queen.

'For anyone who may have an answer,' replied the King. 'Why, even a swineherd would be welcome if he knew what ailed her.'

2

Not All He Could Wish

The King was as good as his word and began advertising that very day. Messengers and heralds were sent scurrying all over the Kingdom of Rivania carrying news-sheets and notices, which were distributed or displayed in town and countryside. The result, however, was far from satisfactory because, despite the proclamations requesting those wise in knowledge of the senses to proceed to the palace, very few responded. This may have been due to the fact that very few had such knowledge or, much more likely, aware of their King's fondness for practical jokes, they concluded this was just such another. Whatever the reason, only very few people waited to see the King and Queen, on a morning a week or so later.

'Show the first one in,' said the King testily to his major-domo.

'Now, Your Majesty?'

'I don't mean next week,' replied the King, and the major-domo bowed himself out.

'Should not the Princess be here too?' asked the Queen.

'I've already sent for her,' replied the King, just as a venerable-looking man was ushered in.

He looked very wise, beneath a crown of snow-white hair, with a large pair of spectacles balanced on his brow. He gazed in silence at the King who gazed silently back. Despite himself the King felt some awe for this scholarly-looking man and wondered how to address him.

'Say something,' whispered the Queen, nudging her husband.

'And who have we here?' said the King.

'Professor at the Central University where I specialise in the involvement of the senses. Are you the patient?' came the reply.

'Of course I'm not,' spluttered the King. 'There's nothing wrong with *my* senses.'

'Then why am I here?' asked the Professor vaguely.

'To attend my daughter, the Princess Kushtu,' replied the King.

'A Princess, you say? Then that should not be difficult,' replied the Professor. 'Is she the lady sitting beside you?'

'That lady is the Queen. The Princess has been sent for,' replied the King, while the Queen hid a smile behind her fan.

Ten minutes later the Princess had still not appeared and the King was finding it difficult to fill in the time. In an attempt to do so he sent for some wine which the Professor refused with a request for water. The water arrived but no Princess.

'Where can that gal have hidden herself?' muttered the King crossly. Because despite all the efforts of numerous servants the Princess had still not been found.

'Perhaps I should go and look for her?' suggested the Queen.

'Perhaps you should,' agreed the King, and gave his attention to watching the Professor setting out mysterious objects on a small table. He breathed an audible sigh of relief when the Queen, at last, appeared with a somewhat dishevelled Princess.

'Well, where did you find her?' asked the

King, whose curiosity outweighed his decorum.

'Hiding up on the battlements,' replied the Queen, and gave her reluctant daughter a push in the direction of the Professor.

'So, this is the young lady?' asked the Professor, peering over his spectacles at the Princess.

'Yes, this is the Princess Kushtu,' corrected the King.

'Well, what seems to be the trouble? What ails you, young lady?' asked the Professor.

'Nothing ails me,' replied Kushtu sulkily.

'It's her sense of humour. She is incapable of

15

laughter or even of smiling,' supplied the King.

'Pity. There must be some deep-rooted cause for such insensibility,' replied the Professor and, picking up a small silver object, began peering into the Princess's eyes. Half an hour later, having examined her eyes, her ears, and her nose, the Professor began packing up his things.

'Well, have you reached a conclusion?' asked the King, who was almost purple in the face by this time because of keeping his emotions in check.

'I have,' replied the Professor. 'I can find nothing wrong with your daughter.'

'You . . . you . . . blockhead,' roared the King, while the Queen did her utmost to calm him. 'Begone from my kingdom and my sight.'

The Professor went from the room as unhurriedly as he had entered it, while the King danced up and down in a rage and the Princess looked on impassively.

'To think I have wasted almost an entire morning only to hear that,' spluttered the King.

'Calm down, my dear, I beg you,' cried the Queen just as another person was ushered in.

He was dressed in black, was much younger

than the Professor, and declared himself to be a crystal-gazer. This was immediately obvious because, having sat down, he stared into a crystal with great concentration. This roused the King's curiosity so much that he went to stand beside him and look into the crystal in his turn.

'Well . . .?' he said some minutes later.

'Sh . . .sh . . . sh,' came the reply.

'We haven't got all day,' said the King.

At last a pronouncement came. 'It is plain to see that the Princess is minus a particular bone, the funny bone,' said the crystal-gazer.

'Balderdash!' cried the King while the Princess fingered each of her elbows in turn just to reassure herself that all was well.

'The crystal never lies,' said the young man.

'Maybe not, but you do,' shouted the King and only just refrained from booting the young man out of the room.

The end of the day came at last but none of the callers, some old and wise, some young and brash, could offer an acceptable solution.

'Is that the last of them?' said the King wearily as the last rays of the sun disappeared over the horizon.

'There's just one more, Your Majesty,' said the major-domo.

'And what does he claim?' asked the King.

'Why, nothing at all, Your Majesty.'

'Then show him in,' said the King.

'To what end, my dear? If he has nothing to offer?' asked the Queen.

'I like his modesty,' replied the King, as into the room came a young man dressed simply in a suit of russet brown.

'Why, Amyas!' exclaimed the Princess.

'You know him?' asked the King.

'He's nought but a lad from the stables,' said the Queen, wrinkling up her nose.

'What brings you here, Amyas? *Inside* the palace?' asked Kushtu.

'I think I might be able to help you,' was the reply.

'In what way, young man?' asked the King.

'In *some* way, Your Majesty. I have had success with sick animals.'

'Yes, he cured my mare of the colic,' put in the Princess.

'And I treated your gun-shy hound,' added Amyas.

'My daughter is not all I could wish, but she falls into neither of those categories,' said the King. 'We merely hope to restore her sense of humour.'

'So I understand, Your Majesty, and in my humble opinion one can only do that by understanding the whole personality.'

'And you believe that to be possible?'

'If I were allowed to spend more time in the company of the Princess, I think I could. At

present I only see her for a few seconds, here and there, when she visits the stables,' replied Amyas.

'Then we shall arrange for you to see more of her,' said the King. 'You can only be an improvement upon the charlatans and mountebanks who have wasted my time today.'

'But husband, a stable lad. Pray think what you are about,' protested the Queen in a whisper.

'A stable lad who shall be promoted. From now on you will be known as the Princess's Protector,' said the King.

3

The Nurse's Story

And so it was that Amyas came to live in the palace. He was given a couple of rooms high up, in one of the corner turrets, where dwelt the Princess's old nurse.

She was very old by this time, but occupied herself in mending and caring for the Princess's clothes. She and Amyas soon became friends, because there was nothing the old woman liked more than to talk about the days when she had charge of the young Princess. Had it not been for her I doubt whether Amyas would have learnt very much about Princess Kushtu because, although always friendly, she remained self-contained and aloof.

As for the Queen, although she could not entirely forget the young man's humble origins, she soon fell under Amyas's spell. And the King – well, of course he had affairs of state to keep him

busy as well as his indulgence in practical jokes.

There were two of which he was particularly fond, one of which was always referred to as 'the tea ceremony'. This usually concerned just one other person and took place in his very private sanctum which was called the King's room. Sometimes it was some minor court official or some visiting personage who would be invited to take tea with the King.

A silver equipage would be carried in ceremoniously and placed before the King, who would then enquire of his guest whether he liked his tea with or without sugar. This would be

followed by a further enquiry as to whether milk was wanted. Having ascertained his guest's preferences the King would then solemnly go through the motions of serving tea but as there was no tea in the pot, no sugar in the basin, or milk in the jug, you can imagine the embarrassment of the guest.

Naturally they were always too polite to point out the deficiencies and would follow the King's example of raising an empty cup to their lips. Whereupon the King would dissolve into laughter, exclaiming between gasps, 'I caught you out there, didn't I?'

However, he always made amends by seeing that his guest was provided with a sumptuous tea before his departure.

Another of his favourite tricks was one employing brightly-coloured paint. A particular chair was reserved for this and was always prepared beforehand.

The unfortunate visitor, having been presented to the King, and well aware of correct court procedure, would walk back a few steps before lowering himself on to the chair provided. So, when a little later, the audience being over, he rose to go he did so to the accompaniment of loud laughter. This was because his bottom bore a colourful design of noughts and crosses, a large sunflower, or sometimes the words 'Kick Me'.

Of course it was an unkind thing to do but even the unfortunate guest came to regard it differently as time went by. His ruined breeches would be shown with pride to his friends as proof of a close relationship with his King.

These, and other such pranks which I may be able to tell you of another time, kept the King happy; but now I must return to Amyas, whom we left in his attic quarters in the turret.

On this particular morning, the Princess having gone to a fitting for a new ballgown, Amyas was sitting with the old nurse who was busy about some ironing.

'Directly this is finished you shall have some soup,' she said.

She was one of those who believed young people needed lots of nourishment.

'Thank you, Nurse,' said Amyas. 'I haven't, so far, made much headway with the Princess. There is scarcely any change since I moved into the palace.'

'And there won't be while she goes on living this kind of life,' replied the old woman.

'Has she always been like this? So solemn and quiet?' asked Amyas.

'Nay, lad. She was as merry a little creature as ever I cared for, once upon a time.'

'Then when did she change?'

'That's what I've been cudgelling my old brains about, trying to remember. I think it all stemmed from one particular birthday party.'

'Why, what happened then?' asked Amyas eagerly.

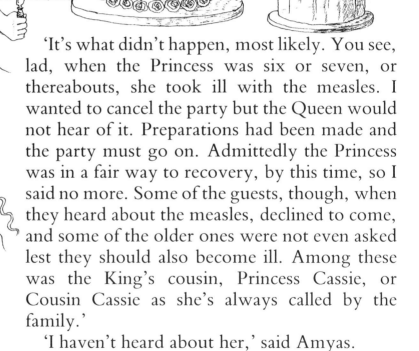

'It's what didn't happen, most likely. You see,
lad, when the Princess was six or seven, or
thereabouts, she took ill with the measles. I
wanted to cancel the party but the Queen would
not hear of it. Preparations had been made and
the party must go on. Admittedly the Princess
was in a fair way to recovery, by this time, so I
said no more. Some of the guests, though, when
they heard about the measles, declined to come,
and some of the older ones were not even asked
lest they should also become ill. Among these
was the King's cousin, Princess Cassie, or
Cousin Cassie as she's always called by the
family.'

'I haven't heard about her,' said Amyas.

'You haven't missed much, lad, for she's a
queer old besom, that one. Well, a day or two

after the party Cousin Cassie arrives, in a fine old state, wanting to know why she was not bidden to the party. The King did his best to explain, so did the Queen, but she paid no heed to either of them and vowed she would get her revenge.'

'And did she?' asked Amyas.

'Who knows, lad? But it was about this time that the Princess lost her sparkle, and went about looking like a little old woman.'

'I see. And you think, you believe, that this Cousin Cassie robbed the Princess of her sense of humour just to repay them?'

'It seems likely. We all know what store the King sets upon a sense of humour, and we all know that story about the wicked fairy who put a curse upon a whole castle of people that sent them to sleep for a hundred years.'

'Have you ever voiced your suspicions to any-one?' asked Amyas.

'Who would pay attention to me?' replied the nurse, and spat viciously on her iron to test its warmth.

'Where does this Cousin Cassie live? I think I might pay her a visit,' Amyas said.

'Only about two days' ride from here, but

don't you tell her I was the one who told you.'

'Of course not,' said Amyas, and went in search of the Princess.

He found her sitting beside a pool, where a fountain played, watching the goldfish gliding to and fro.

'Ah! there you are,' said Amyas.

The Princess lifted her head but made no other sign that she had heard him.

'I want to go and see your Cousin Cassie,' he said.

'Whatever do you want to do that for?'

'Because she might be the one who robbed you of your sense of humour,' Amyas told her.

'But how could she do a thing like that? And for what reason?' asked the Princess.

'How she did it I do not know,' replied Amyas. 'Senses are unlike anything else in that they have no shape, no substance. Nothing like a tooth which, if it fell out, would leave a gap in your mouth or like a lock of hair, which would immediately be missed.' Here he gazed admiringly at the Princess's abundant brown tresses before continuing. 'Somehow or other she must have spirited it away.'

'But what possible reason could she have?' asked the Princess.

Amyas shrugged, not wanting to betray the old nurse's confidence. ''Tis said that she bears you a grudge.'

'That, at least, is true,' agreed the Princess, 'although our family is not alone in that. She cares very little for anyone and scarcely ever ventures out.'

'When did you see her last?' asked Amyas.

'That I cannot tell you. Not for many years, I think.'

'But you know where she lives? You can tell me where to find her?'

'I can do better than that. I will take you there,' replied the Princess, who thought it would be a welcome change to escape from court etiquette by riding into the countryside.

'But would the King allow it?' asked Amyas, who thought that something like this was just what the Princess needed.

'Just leave it to me. I can usually persuade my father to do exactly what I want,' replied the Princess.

'Gladly,' agreed Amyas.

4

Cousin Cassie

And so it was that, a few days afterwards, Amyas and the Princess took their leave of the King and Queen and set out on a journey that was to last much longer than any of them could have foreseen.

The Princess had been quite right in stating that the King would agree to her request. Directly he heard of their wanting to visit Cousin Cassie, he gave them his full support – provided only that the Princess travelled incognito.

Maybe you're not quite sure what 'incognito' means? Well, it's a term much used by royalty, and other important people, when they want to travel abroad without being recognised. To ensure this they dress themselves differently and use false names.

'But surely they should take someone with them?' suggested the Queen who did not fancy the idea. 'A maid or two at the very least?'

'That would defeat the whole object,' said the King. 'It's about time our daughter discovered how the rest of the world lives.'

'But she has never been called upon even to dress herself, and knows absolutely nothing about preparing or serving a meal,' continued the Queen.

'Then now is the time for her to find out,' said the King.

'If you are really sure?'

'Of course I'm sure. In any case they will be gone for only four or five days,' returned the King.

It was then that Amyas made his suggestion that the Princess should dress up as a man. 'No-one then will have the slightest idea who she really is,' he said.

A sparkle appeared in Kushtu's eyes, which did not escape the King. 'A very good idea,' he said.

And so it was that on the day following two young men were seen to ride out from the palace mounted upon two sturdy moorland ponies. No-one paid them any attention except for the

King and Queen who watched discreetly from
an upstairs window, until the pair rode out of
sight. The Princess's braids had been wound
round her head and covered by a jaunty green cap
which matched her cloak.

'Are you quite comfortable?' Amyas asked
her.

'Quite,' replied the Princess, and urged her
little pony into a faster pace.

Very soon they left the main highway by a
little bridge to take the road through a forest
where the birds were busy, building nests, and
little groups of deer watched their passing without themselves being seen.

They had lunch beside a pond covered in

water-lilies, in the company of a group of children who were happy to part with their rather plain fare in exchange for some of the delicacies from Amyas's picnic basket.

'What are you all doing here?' the Princess asked them.

'Having a holiday from school. It's lessons again tomorrow,' she was told.

'Enjoy your holiday then,' cried the Princess as, presently, she and Amyas rode away, to a chorus of farewells.

They spent the night at a wayside inn, where rooms had been reserved for them, and it was not until late the following afternoon that they clattered into the little country town on the edge of which lived Princess Cassie.

The house turned out to be somewhat small, for a Princess, and stood in the middle of a large garden surrounded by a high brick wall. Leaving the ponies tied up outside they entered through a tall iron gate, which creaked rustily, into an overgrown garden where flowers and shrubs and trees grew happily together.

'I think that is she,' said the Princess, disregarding the front door, which stood open, and pointing to a distant figure surrounded by a ring of beehives.

'How do you know?' asked Amyas, because from that distance it was impossible to see whether it was man or woman, young or old, that they were looking at. A large straw hat and a thick black veil masked most of what was underneath it.

'I don't know, but I've heard she keeps bees,' said the Princess as they halted just outside the ring of hives.

'Well, don't stand gaping there. Come and help me put this lid on the hive,' a voice said from beneath the hat.

'You go. I daren't,' whispered Kushtu.

Amyas obeyed, although somewhat reluctantly. He knew very little about bees.

'They won't sting you. Hold this lid while I tuck in this bit of blanket,' she said.

Amyas took the top of the hive from her and, after she had tucked the blanket carefully into place, so as not to crush any bees, helped her replace it. Bees were coming and going into most of the hives but paid little or no attention to the watchers.

'Tea should be ready now,' remarked Princess
Cassie, and led the way towards the house without even a glance at Princess Kushtu.

'Are you not curious as to who we are and why
we have come?' asked Amyas.

'Not particularly. You can tell me, should you
want to, over tea,' was the reply.

Tea was laid out upon a little round table on
the terrace.

35

'Sit down, both of you. I shan't be long,' said Cousin Cassie, and disappeared inside the house to reappear a little later minus her hat, veil and gloves.

'Who's going to be mother?' she said.

'I will,' said Kushtu, and began to pour out.

'Good. So who might you be, then? Don't recollect we've ever met before.'

'Oh yes, we have. I'm the only child of your cousin, the King,' replied Kushtu.

'Now I know you for an imposter. He had but one child and she a daughter. Besides, she's little more than a child,' replied Cassie, folding a thin piece of bread and butter into a lump, and cramming it into her mouth.

'I *am* that daughter, travelling incognito, and Amyas here is my protector,' Kushtu said, and snatched off her cap, allowing her thick brown braids to fall over her shoulders.

'Bless my solitary years! How you've grown, then. But what are you doing here? I've had absolutely no communication with the Palace for a very long time,' Cassie told them.

'Whose fault is that?' asked Kushtu.

'You know very well whose fault it is. That

ridiculous man, your father, slighted me dread-
fully. I shall never be able to forgive him.'

'Nor forget either, it seems,' said Amyas.

'Who asked for your opinion?' asked Cassie.

'No-one, but I think you should know what
brings us here.'

'And what does bring you here?'

'The Princess's sense of humour, or lack of it.
It was you who stole it, was it not?' said Amyas.

'Who says so?'

'That matters little. Why did you?' asked
Amyas.

'Because I was not invited to the birthday
party. I stole it in a fit of temper and was sorry
afterwards.'

'The reason you were not invited was only to
protect you from an attack of measles,' explained
Kushtu.

'But I had had the measles. I needed no protection – and I receive so few invitations,' said
Cassie.

'Just tell us what you did with it, and all will be
well,' said Amyas.

'It's always been quite safe,' said Cassie.

'Yes, but where?' asked Kushtu.

'The last place we put it was in a tree,' said Cassie.

'But why a tree?' asked Kushtu.

'To keep it fresh,' said Cassie, and led them out to the orchard where daffodils raised their heads above the long grass.

'Which tree? There are so many here,' cried Kushtu.

'In that old cherry tree, in the corner,' Cassie told her.

It was indeed an old cherry tree whose shiny red bark was peeling away in several places. Some branches had been broken off by the wind and lay rotting in the grass beneath, while a few white flowers shone out like stars.

Pointing to a small round hole about halfway up the tree, and just above a stout branch Cassie said, 'It's in there.'

'I'll go and get it,' said Amyas, and began to climb.

'It can't be very big to fit in there. What exactly does it look like?' asked Kushtu curiously.

'I don't know. How can you describe a sense of humour?' replied Cassie vaguely.

'There's nothing in here,' shouted Amyas,

whose fingers had explored the hole in vain.

'There must be,' cried Cassie, wringing her hands. 'Are you quite sure?'

'Quite sure,' Amyas replied, as he dropped down beside them.

'What can have happened to it?' asked Kushtu.

'It . . . it . . . must have been stolen,' replied Cassie.

'But who would want it?' asked Kushtu.

'The yaffle, to be sure,' replied Cassie.

'What makes you say that?' asked Amyas.

'Because only the yaffle knew about it. It was he who put it there and promised to guard it,' explained Cassie.

'Whatever is a yaffle?' asked Kushtu.

'Heavens, girl, don't you know anything?' cried Cassie.

'It's a kind of woodpecker, a green woodpecker,' said Amyas. 'Where is he now, Princess?'

'Goodness knows. He flew south weeks ago,' replied Princess Cassie.

5

In Search of the Yaffle

It was a very sad Princess who helped Amyas stable the ponies some time later.

'What can we do now?' she asked.

'Go in search of that yaffle, I suppose. It should not be too difficult because they are colourful birds, and very noisy.'

'But what will my father say?'

'Who knows? We shall not be there to hear, shall we?' replied Amyas mischievously.

'Then where will we be?' asked Kushtu, whose spirits had risen rapidly upon hearing that their journey was not yet over.

'Riding south, to be sure,' replied Amyas, and added an extra supply of oats to the ponies' supper.

'I wonder what the yaffle could possibly want with a sense of humour?' asked Kushtu as they were sitting round the supper table.

'For one purpose only,' replied Cousin Cassie.

'And what would that be?' asked Kushtu.

'Have you never heard a woodpecker laugh?' asked Cousin Cassie.

'Never,' replied Kushtu.

'Well, it's not much of a laugh, truth to tell. It's my belief that that bird, who is a conceited kind of creature, took your sense of humour in the vain hope that it would improve his call. Now I come to think back, he scarcely ever left that tree, after hiding it, but sat there, yaff-yaff-yaffling, day after day.'

'And you never suspected anything?' asked Amyas.

'Not until now. I merely thought he was guarding it well,' said Cousin Cassie wryly.

'Well, we shall just have to go and look for him,' said Amyas.

'By riding south, you mean?'

'By riding south,' agreed Amyas before biting into a juicy pear.

'But that would mean you having to cross the desert,' said Cousin Cassie.

'And why shouldn't we cross the desert?' asked Amyas.

'It's easy enough if you happen to be a bird, but quite a different matter if you're on foot,' Cassie told him.

'We have the ponies,' Kushtu reminded her.

'What I don't understand is why you have to go at all,' objected Cassie.

'It's very simple, Cousin. To regain my sense of humour.'

'Is that so important? You seem perfectly well to me.'

'But not to my father,' said Kushtu.

'Oh, your father! He always did have an exaggerated idea about the importance of a sense of humour,' said Cassie.

'I agree,' said Amyas.

They went on talking about humour, and what makes people laugh, until it was almost dark and they could barely distinguish each other's faces.

'It's high time we were all in bed. I gave instructions for rooms to be prepared for you both, so come, child,' said Cousin Cassie to Kushtu, and led the way upstairs, while Amyas went out to assure himself that the ponies had settled down for the night.

The following morning was entirely taken up with preparations for the journey. The cook and her kitchen-maid busied themselves baking lots of pasties and pies while the gardener sorted over last year's apples to select the sounder ones. Cousin Cassie, who had begun by opposing the whole scheme, suddenly changed her mind and became most enthusiastic about it, insisting upon their taking the most unsuitable items, like sugar-plums and honeycomb.

'No more, I beg you,' said Amyas. 'We have almost more than we can carry already.'

'Nonsense. There's nothing like honey for giving one energy,' and she thrust both packages down the side of a bulging sack.

The ponies stood still patiently while their unfamiliar burdens were loaded on.

'They won't be able to carry us as well,' objected Kushtu.

'No, we shall have to walk. For a while, at least,' said Amyas.

'You will let my father know we have had to go on, Cousin Cassie?' Kushtu said, just as they were setting off.

'But not where,' added Amyas. 'We don't

want a search party sent after us.'

'I understand. Take good care of the Princess,' she replied.

'I will. I am her Protector, after all,' Amyas said.

It took two whole days, after their leave-taking with Cousin Cassie, to bring them to the desert. There it was, a vast expanse, stretching away to the horizon. By that time their provisions had lessened sufficiently to be carried by one pony so that Kushtu could ride again.

'It looks rather frightening,' she said, staring out over the undulating expanse with its purple shadows.

'And exciting too,' said Amyas. 'Let us spend the night here, under this palm tree, and set off early tomorrow.'

'It's really quite cold,' said Kushtu, beginning to shiver. 'I thought deserts were always hot.'

'They usually are, in the daytime. It's the nights that are cold,' Amyas told her. 'So, you set out the supper and I will do my best to light a fire.'

It was only a little fire he made but it was most comforting as it burned away merrily. By the

time supper was over, and the ponies fed, the fire had almost burned itself out for lack of fuel. Even so it still gave out a little heat as they huddled together beside it.

'We'll just have to keep each other warm,' said Amyas, moving closer to the Princess.

'You do look funny, Amyas,' she replied, seeing the sooty streak on the side of his face, in the light of the flickering fire.

'I must, indeed, if it makes you smile, which is something I've longed to see you do,' replied Amyas.

'Shall I do it again?'

'It's an accomplishment well worth cultivating,' he replied, smiling in his turn.

But despite all her efforts, and many grimaces, Kushtu could not repeat it.

'I can't,' she said sadly.

'No, smiles almost always come unbidden, but you've made a start,' said Amyas.

6

The Sandstorm

It was while they were finishing their lunch on the following day that they were joined by the strangest of visitors. He came ambling slowly towards them over the sand, casting his long nose from side to side.

'Whatever is it?' whispered Kushtu, clutching Amyas's arm.

'I don't know,' he replied, adding, as the creature began sniffing at some crumbs, 'It's quite harmless, I'm sure.'

The ponies evidently agreed, as after briefly raising their heads they soon began eating again.

'Perhaps it's hungry,' suggested Kushtu.

'Indeed I am,' replied their unexpected visitor, and went on to tell them that he was an armadillo who had had very little to eat for several days. This was because, due to an eye injury, he could see with only one eye.

'Oh, you poor thing. Come close, pray do,
and let me dress it for you,' cried Kushtu, and
took from her pocket a small jar of salve which
Cousin Cassie had assured her would cure
almost anything. The armadillo, reassured by
that gentle voice, did as she asked, enabling

48

Kushtu to clean the eye and apply the salve.

'It feels better already,' he said, shaking his head.

'Then come and eat your fill,' Amyas invited him, spreading out a variety of fare. 'We have more than enough.'

The armadillo immediately began tasting most of the things set out before him, before deciding which of them he preferred when he settled down to eat in earnest, but always in a most delicate manner.

'Have you travelled far?' Amyas asked him presently.

'Far enough,' he replied. 'And you, you don't belong to the desert?'

'No, we've come in search of a green wood-pecker or yaffle as he's often called. You have not seen him, I suppose?'

'I may have done although I have little interest in birds. However, I have heard tell there's a wood, at the fringe of the desert, where birds are accustomed to foregather before making their crossing.'

'Is it far, do you know?' asked Kushtu.

'It depends how you travel. With horses it

should not be difficult,' replied the armadillo, while shaking himself free of the crumbs that had lodged among the little scales encasing his body.

'You carry quite an armour,' said Amyas.

'Yes, it is my main protection. Proof against almost anything except a jaguar,' he replied somewhat smugly.

'This wood you mentioned – in what direction does it lie?' asked Amyas.

'North, north-east, I believe,' replied the armadillo vaguely, and pointed with his long nose.

'And will you go with us to show us the way?' asked Amyas.

'My pace is not yours, but perhaps we shall meet again,' replied the armadillo abruptly and off he went, in the direction he had just indicated.

'What an odd little creature,' Kushtu said. 'Shall we follow him?'

Amyas shrugged. 'One direction seems as good as any other,' he replied and began to re-load the ponies. Without the sun, which had long disappeared, he had lost all sense of direction.

The armadillo had quickly disappeared from sight although they were able to follow his tracks for some little while, until they were hidden by drifting sand.

'How very dark it has grown,' said Kushtu, who was riding just ahead of Amyas and the baggage pony.

'So it has,' agreed Amyas. 'And my pony has developed a limp, so let us look for a suitable place to stop.'

They soon found one in a convenient hollow, where they unsaddled the ponies and settled down. Neither of them was hungry and they sat, side by side, in a friendly silence.

Presently: 'Tell me about your early life, Amyas. I know almost nothing about you,' said Kushtu.

So Amyas told her about his early years that had been spent aboard his father's ship – his father was a sea captain. They made regular voyages, over the inland seas, carrying both passengers and freight among the various islands. The captain also conducted important dealings for some of the merchants whose goods he carried. One of these merchants, who was devoted to Amyas, succeeded in persuading the captain into allowing his son to spend the summer with him, in his holiday home, where the mornings would be spent in study and the rest of the day in leisure.

The captain readily agreed and set out on a voyage from which, sadly, he was not to return. The ship foundered in a storm and went down with all hands. So Amyas remained with the wealthy merchant, who treated him like a son, until the merchant was taken ill and died suddenly, in a foreign city. Thus Amyas was left all alone in the world, with little money and less knowledge of how to support himself. Eventually he came to Rivania where, in its capital city, he heard there was work to be had in the royal stables.

'I offered my services, and you know the rest,' Amyas said.

Kushtu had been so engrossed in listening to this story that it was only now that it was over she saw how dark and windy it had become.

'Whatever's happening?' she cried as a gust of wind wrenched at her cap and showers of sand whipped her cheeks.

'It must be a sandstorm. Quick, help me with
the ponies,' said Amyas.

The two sturdy little ponies were trembling,
and on the verge of panic, as whirling sand filled
the air, blocking their nostrils and almost blind-
ing them.

Kushtu did her best to comply, but the wind and the frightened ponies proved too strong for her and she fell to the ground. Fortunately Amyas was able to grab the ponies just in time and pull them down beside the fallen Princess. Here they all huddled together until at long last the storm was over.

By that time the night was well advanced and when at last a pale dawn arrived, and they could see again, the landscape had subtly changed. What had looked like distant hills had now merged into the plain, and the hollow that had given them some shelter was a shelving bank.

'How are the ponies?' croaked Kushtu as she sat up and, with her kerchief, began wiping grains of sand from eyes and nose.

'In very poor shape,' replied Amyas, shaking his head vigorously and blinking his sore eyes.

'Perhaps if we were to give them a drink?' she suggested.

'Of what? All our baggage has disappeared,' cried Amyas, who was plunging about, unsuccessfully, in the shifting sand.

'Are you quite sure?' asked Kushtu, joining in the search.

'Of course I'm sure,' replied Amyas, whose hands were now scratched and bleeding from burrowing in the sand.

'Oh! your poor hands. And is there nothing for us either?'

'Nothing at all.'

'Then what are we going to do?' asked Kushtu, who felt very much like crying, except that her eyes were as dry as everything else.

'We begin walking,' said Amyas gruffly.

'I don't think I can,' she replied.

'We have no choice, Princess,' Amyas told her.

He knew very well that no-one can exist for very long in a desert without water. 'Come along,' he said encouragingly and, giving her the bridle of one pony to hold, led the other up the bank.

There was little Kushtu could do except follow him.

7

Help – of a Kind

Fortunately they did not have to travel far before help came, by which time both Kushtu and Amyas were practically exhausted, and the ponies in a sad way.

'Look!' said Amyas pointing a shaking hand. 'Someone's coming.'

Kushtu raised her head and saw what she first thought to be a string of horses coming towards them. This turned out to be a line of camels in charge of a man and a boy. The boy was apparently young and very small, but he darted about, from one end of the line to the other, encouraging the slow and restraining the eager camels. The man remained almost immobile, riding the leading camel until, catching sight of the two weary travellers, he dismounted and came unhurriedly towards them. He had darting black eyes, a glossy black moustache which hung down, in two rat's tails, on either side of his chin, baggy trousers, and an odd-looking hat. The boy came to stand close behind him, peering up eagerly at the strangers.

'You seem to be in trouble,' the man said.

'Pray, can you give us some water?' Amyas pleaded.

The man made a sign to the boy who ran to one of the camels and came back carrying a flask.

Kushtu drank first before passing it on to Amyas. Although the water was warm, she thought it the most wonderful drink she had ever had and the few drops that dribbled down her chin she pursued, eagerly, with her tongue.

'Have you come far?' asked the man whose name, they were told, was Crukhid.

'Far enough,' replied Amyas. 'We were caught in a sandstorm and lost all our baggage.'

'Those beasts of yours are not used to the desert, I see.'

'No. May we give them a drink too?'

The man shook his head while his roving eyes took in the silver mountings on the ponies' bridles and the richness of Kushtu's clothes, still apparent through their coating of sand.

'Sorry, lad. We have only enough for our own
needs.'

'But our ponies will die unless they have water
soon.'

'Aye, they will.'

'And yet you refuse to help them?' asked
Kushtu.

'I did not refuse help. What I propose is that we
do a trade. *Your* two ponies for one of my finest

and fastest camels,' replied Crukhid.

'Oh no, we could not part with them,' replied Kushtu.

'Then they will surely die, and you with them,' said Crukhid.

'He's probably right,' said Amyas sadly, because the ponies were a sorry sight with their drooping heads and lack-lustre eyes.

'We'll treat them well,' Crukhid told them. 'See how fat and healthy our camels are, how glossy their coats.'

This was certainly true.

'But what about water? You said you had only enough for your own needs,' replied Kushtu.

'But one camel less, should you take one,' Crukhid reminded them. 'And provided each camel is given a little less there will be sufficient for the ponies. At least until we reach the oasis.'

'I think we should accept. We really have no choice,' said Amyas.

'Is it far to this oasis?' asked Kushtu.

'You can do better than that. The camel I will give you is trained to return home. In little more than an hour you will arrive in my village, where hospitality of a most generous kind awaits you.'

'Very well,' said Kushtu, while the small boy, who seemed able to obey his master's orders without words being spoken, came towards them leading a pure white camel with enormous dark eyes.

'Isn't she a beauty?' asked Crukhid fondly.

They had to agree she was, and after being helped into the saddle were soon moving along at a brisk pace.

Kushtu had no heart to bid the ponies farewell and neither of them dared to look back. The camel's gait, they found, was very different from that of the ponies and, to begin with, they had all they could do not to fall off.

The desert landscape was subtly changing, with clumps of coarse grass interspersed among spiky shrubs. Presently they saw ahead of them what appeared to be a vast encampment where, to their immense relief, were green growing things, and people moving about among the tents. Their camel had quickened her pace and so brought them into the centre of this strangest of places where she came to an abrupt halt. Their sudden arrival had alerted the rest of the inhabitants, some of whom began crowding around to watch their descent from the camel. Almost immediately a man stepped out from the rest who looked not unlike Crukhid and had an authoritative manner. After directing a by-stander to take charge of the camel he approached the strangers and said, 'Did Crukhid send you here?'

'Yes, he did. He said you would give us food and rest,' replied Amyas.

'And so we shall. Come with me,' replied the man.

He led them between lines of tents to one slightly larger than the rest, and at the end of a long line. A carpet covered most of the floor.

'Wait here,' he said, and disappeared.

In a very little while an attendant appeared, bringing a bowl of clear water and cloths for them to wash themselves. He was shortly fol-lowed by another bringing food and drink. After this they were left alone.

'I wonder what will happen next?' asked Kushtu, when they had eaten and drunk their fill.

'We can only wait and see,' replied Amyas. 'Maybe they can direct us to that wood the armadillo told us about.'

He had scarcely finished speaking when the man who had brought them to the tent reappeared. 'I am bidden to take you to our ruler,' he said.

It was already dark but fires flickered, outside the tents, where preparations went on for the evening meal. Their way led them beside a broad lake beyond which were more tents backed by tall trees.

'This way,' said their guide, who was a man of few words, and he ushered them into a large tent where richly glowing carpets hung like tapestries on the walls, and covered most of the floor. At the far end stood two men, one on each side of a throne-like chair, each holding a flaring torch which illuminated that end of the tent. They had barely absorbed all this when there entered a most impressive figure followed by a few companions. He was dressed entirely in white, and as he took his seat jewels in his ears and upon his fingers shone in the torchlight.

'I understand that Crukhid sent you to me,' was his only greeting. 'With one of his camels.'

'Which we traded for two ponies,' replied Amyas.

'And where were you bound on these ponies?'

'You might call it a fruitless mission,' replied Amyas who had reluctantly reached this conclusion. 'However, we would like to thank you for your timely hospitality.'

'For which you will be well rewarded,' added Kushtu, choosing to ignore Amyas's attempt to silence her. He hurried on: 'And now we would be most grateful if you could supply us with suitable mounts to take us home.'

'That, unfortunately, I cannot do,' came the

reply. 'As you may have seen, my people are many, and have barely enough for their own needs. What I propose to do therefore is . . .'

'My father is the King of Rivania. He will pay you well for our safe return,' interrupted Kushtu.

'Indeed he will, young man,' came the swift reply. 'Nevertheless we are grateful to have your assurance.'

'So, when may we leave?' asked Kushtu anxiously.

'Directly we receive your ransom,' he replied. 'Meantime you will be well cared for.'

'But you can't keep us here against our will,' protested Amyas.

'Oh, but I can! Tomorrow you will be taken to more suitable quarters. Meantime, I wish you goodnight.'

So saying he rose and, followed by his retinue, left the tent without giving them a chance to say more.

8

The Rescue

'This is all my fault, isn't it?' said Kushtu.

Both she and Amyas had been taken back to the smaller tent where they were to spend the night.

Any thoughts they had of escaping were soon dismissed because of the two guards just outside the entrance to the tent. They could hear, from time to time, their guttural voices and occasional laughter.

'It was because I told them who my father was,' Kushtu continued. 'Had I not done so we might, even now, be on our way home.'

'I doubt it, Princess,' replied Amyas softly. 'I suspect that they detain many unwary travellers who are either robbed or held to ransom. They have become very skilful at it, judging by the jewels worn by our captors.'

'How long will it be before my father receives

news of our plight?' asked Kushtu.

'Not many days,' replied Amyas. 'I am glad I shall not be there when he does.'

'He may be cross but he won't refuse to pay the ransom, will he?' Kushtu asked anxiously.

'Of course not. You are very dear to him. But what he will do about me is a very different matter. Not only have I failed to protect you, but we are no nearer finding your sense of humour,' replied Amyas gloomily.

'You could not have foreseen a sandstorm – which is why we are here. Besides, I want you to know that I would not have missed this adventure for anything in the wide, wide world. I have enjoyed it all,' replied Kushtu.

'Even the sandstorm?'

'Even the sandstorm,' agreed Kushtu, not quite truthfully, but it made Amyas feel a whole lot better.

'I think, perhaps, we ought to try and sleep now,' he said and, putting an arm about Kushtu, offered her his shoulder for a pillow.

There was almost complete silence and darkness within the tent save for the murmurs of the guards, a distant cough from a camel, or the wailing cry of a child. Very soon though, despite these alien sounds, Kushtu's breathing became so regular that Amyas judged her to be asleep. He was just about to follow her example when he heard a faint, indefinable, sound from the far end of the tent.

Cautiously he sat up as the sound was repeated. He strained his eyes to pierce the darkness and was rewarded by seeing a jagged split in the stout canvas which widened even as he looked at it. Through it could be seen one or two stars twinkling in the night sky.

Someone or something had pierced the wall of the tent!

'Who is it? Who's there?' he whispered, anxious not to rouse the guards.

'It is I,' came the hoarse reply, and through the slit was thrust the sharp nose of the armadillo,

followed, almost immediately, by its entire body. 'Not a sound,' he said and, with his sharp claws, began enlarging the gap.

Meanwhile Amyas had roused Kushtu, who sat up and was wide awake in an instant.

'Follow me,' muttered the armadillo, and disappeared through the slit he had made, closely followed by the other two.

'However did you find us?' whispered Kushtu, who could contain her curiosity no longer.

'Not a sound, if you please,' came the swift and stern reply from the little armadillo.

They strove to obey him as he led them away from the tents, skirting the ashes of smouldering fires, towards a faint track which wound among bushes that were only just visible, as a dark mass in the pervading darkness. The only light came from the stars high above them.

Although the armadillo had very short legs he nevertheless travelled quite quickly, and soon the encampment was left behind. Much as they longed to know how and why this small creature had found them, they forbore to question him further until they came to a halt in the shelter of some rocks shading a deep well, just as dawn was breaking. They were all very thirsty, and it was not until their thirst was satisfied that the armadillo was ready to talk.

'How did you know where we were?' asked Kushtu.

'I saw your meeting with Crukhid, but did nothing to help you,' replied the armadillo.

'But what could you have done?' asked Amyas.

'Very little then, which is why I seek to make amends now,' replied the armadillo. 'It was largely because I gave you the wrong directions that you fell in with that villain.'

'I see,' replied Amyas.

'However, my powers are restricted, because of my size, which is why I enlisted The Great One. He and I have made a pact,' continued the armadillo grandly.

'What kind of pact?' asked Amyas.

'You will soon see, because here he comes,' replied the armadillo, for walking towards them was an enormous elephant, which looked more and more frightening the nearer it came.

'How big it is!' gasped Kushtu, drawing closer to Amyas.

'Have no fear. I arranged this meeting,' said the armadillo.

'To what end?' asked Amyas.

'Is this the couple you told me about?' asked the elephant, waving his big ears backwards and forwards.

'Won't one of you tell us what your intentions are?' begged Amyas, who, while acknowledging the animal's goodwill, was impelled to know more.

'Tampala has agreed to take you to a place of safety,' said the armadillo.

'But why? Why do this for us?' asked Amyas.

'Because I asked him,' replied the armadillo.

'And because Crukhid and his like are no friends of mine,' added the elephant. 'Now, mount up, both of you, and let us waste no more time.' Both Amyas and Kushtu were only too ready to comply but had no idea how to do so. The big body towered above them like a cliff. Tampala was plainly getting impatient but there were no handholds anywhere in that thick hide.

'They need *some* help, Tampala,' said the armadillo.

'Then why not say so?' replied Tampala testily

and, seizing Kushtu round the waist with his
trunk, bore her aloft. She managed to suppress
her fear and, while settling herself in the slight
hollow behind that enormous head, watched
Amyas, being carried up to sit beside her.

'Now, where shall I take you?' asked
Tampala.

'I would like to go home. Home to Rivania,'
said Kushtu.

'And so you shall. What else *can* we do?' said
Amyas.

'Then hold on tight,' said Tampala, and set off briskly without giving them a chance to bid the armadillo farewell.

It had not been easy riding on a camel, even with a saddle, but it was much more difficult riding upon the bare back of an elephant. Finally they found the temerity each to grasp hold of an ear, when things went rather better. Tampala seemed not to mind, and without any sign of haste carried them along at a brisk pace. Even so, it was very far from comfortable because the sun blazed down and flies buzzed about their heads. Kushtu was thinking wistfully of her soft bed, back home in the palace, while Amyas felt slightly sick.

'Is it much further?' he asked desperately.

It seemed Tampala had not heard, so Amyas bent lower and repeated his question right into the elephant's ear.

'Look over to the west. There you will see some trees, which make a popular resting place for all those about to cross the desert. That is where I shall leave you to make your own way,' replied Tampala.

And there, not far away, and growing clearer

every moment, was a wood of shady trees and green, green grass. As they drew closer they could hear the calling of birds and saw what they thought was a spotted deer disappearing among the trees.

'We shall never be able to thank you for what you have done,' said Amyas to Tampala, after they had dismounted by the simple means of sliding to the ground.

'There is no need. To thwart Crukhid and all his tribe, in any way I can, is reward enough for me and compensates for their treatment of many of my people,' replied Tampala.

So saying, he tossed his great head, and set off back the way they had come.

9

Found – at Last

For some little while after Tampala had left they sat perfectly still exulting in the blessed shade and luxuriant growth all around them. Birds sang gaily or flitted about among the trees, while busy rustlings in the undergrowth reminded them they were not alone.

Then, because by this time they were both hungry and thirsty, they roused themselves to begin picking the various fruits that grew there in abundance before drinking from a sparkling stream. It was while they were dangling their feet in the cool water that Kushtu said, 'I wish we might stay here for ever and ever.'

'That's not possible, Princess. Clothes wear out and winter comes,' Amyas said.

'Together with colic and chilblains,' replied Kushtu.

'So let us make the most of today because our

time together grows very short,' responded Amyas.

'Why do you say that?' asked Kushtu.

'Because I've failed in what I set out to do. We have not found your sense of humour. It will be back to the stables for me.'

'And would that matter so very much?'

'Of course it would. I think I have loved you from the very first moment that I saw you.'

'And when was that?'

'You came riding into the stable-yard, one fine morning, on your little white mare,' Amyas said.

'I don't remember,' said Kushtu, although she did.

'And I shall never forget, although I could not imagine then that I should be fortunate enough to spend so many days in your company. But that is why I presented myself to the King, hoping I might be able to restore your sense of humour.'

'And you think you have failed?' asked Kushtu.

'I know I have. When did I ever hear you laugh? Besides, not only did I drag you on a wild-goose chase – or should I say yaffle chase? – but when the King hears, as he undoubtedly will, that you were held to ransom, even for a few days, he'll have no more time for me.'

'Oh, surely not,' cried Kushtu vehemently. 'Because I think I love you, too.'

'Then you must forget me. What has a stable lad to offer a Princess?' replied Amyas.

'All that I shall ever want. Life is real only when I'm with you.'

'We have no choice in the matter,' Amyas told her sadly.

It was at that moment that a hollow tapping sound could be heard, and he raised his hand for silence.

'What is it?' whispered Kushtu.

'Listen!' he replied, while a look of surprise and satisfaction spread slowly over his face as the series of taps was repeated again and again.

'Whatever is it?' Kushtu asked again.

'It seems we have finally discovered the wood the armadillo talked about. And we have wandered all over the desert and back to do it,' he said.

'And is that really the yaffle I can hear?' asked Kushtu.

'I believe so. Come, let's go and see,' he replied, hastily pulling on his boots.

They did not have to go far before they came to a solitary pine tree. Here a black and white bird, with patches of crimson, was busy drumming with his beak, halfway up the tree. Hearing their approach it ceased its drumming and hopped up the trunk to perch on a severed branch where it turned to face them.

'It's very pretty,' said Kushtu.

'But not the bird we're looking for. It's not a yaffle,' he replied, and added, "Good-day to you, woodpecker.'

'And to you,' replied the bird.

'We heard you tapping and mistook you for a yaffle,' Amyas said.

'Many folk make the same mistake,' replied the woodpecker. 'It's quite understandable as we're closely related.'

'Are there any yaffles in these parts, do you know?' asked Amyas.

'Yes, there's a pair that took up residence in this very wood not so long ago,' replied the woodpecker.

'Do tell us where?'

'There's a group of lime trees just beyond the stream. That is where I saw them last,' replied the woodpecker, and straightway resumed his drumming.

They soon found the lime trees and almost immediately noticed a large greenish-coloured bird busy about the base of one of them. It too had touches of crimson.

'Look there . . . there he is,' whispered Amyas, who hardly dared hope that this could be the yaffle they had travelled so far to find.

'Then speak to him,' begged Kushtu. 'Before he flies away.'

'I can't think what to say,' responded Amyas ruefully and then, raising his voice, 'Hallo, there,' he called.

The yaffle's only response was to fly up into the tree.

'We . . . we were told we might find you here,' Amyas continued.

'And now you have found me, what then?' the yaffle replied.

'We . . . er . . . we're wondering if you've ever been in Rivania,' said Amyas.

'Often. Most of my life has been spent there.'

'In what part?'

'That's more difficult. I know *where*, but not its name.'

'Would it be anywhere near the Princess Cassie's place, perhaps?' asked Amyas, sensing that, at last, they had found their quarry.

'It would. I return there every year. To the orchard, to be exact.'

'Then perhaps you can tell us what was hidden in a certain cherry tree?'

'Oh, that!' replied the yaffle, fluttering his wings, and half-closing his eyelids.

'Yes, that!' replied Amyas.

'It all happened some long time ago . . .'

'Not so long. What became of it?'

'I have it still. It's quite safe,' replied the yaffle.

'So you *did* take my sense of humour?' said Kushtu.

'What else could I do when I had promised to guard it? The old woman had forgotten all about it, and I needed to go south. I have returned with it safely every year.'

'She thought you had stolen it to improve your laughter,' said Kushtu.

'What nonsense! There's nothing wrong with that,' cried the yaffle and, lifting up his head, gave his familiar call.

'No, indeed!' agreed Amyas. 'You're in excellent voice. So perhaps you will now return it to its rightful owner?'

'Oh, is it yours?' replied the yaffle, and flew up into the tree to return, a few seconds later, with what looked like a glass marble, which he let fall among the grass.

'I never imagined it would look like this,' said Kushtu and, kneeling down, parted the grass fronds to allow the sunlight through. 'It's just like a soap bubble,' she added, entranced by the pretty colours and, with finger and thumb, sought to pick it up.

'And, just like a bubble, it's burst,' said Amyas.

And it had, without leaving a trace.

'But where is it . . .? I don't understand,' cried Kushtu, looking about her anxiously.

'You must have absorbed it, Princess. There's no other explanation,' said Amyas.

'But I don't look or feel any different,' replied Kushtu, examining each of her fingers in turn.

'You will, in time,' said Amyas confidently and turned to the yaffle who, perched upon a branch, was watching them curiously. 'Knowing Rivania as you do, will you be so good as to direct us there?' he asked.

'You're almost at the border. Just travel on northwards, keeping the sun always on your left.'

'I understand,' said Amyas and, taking Kushtu's hand, set off in the direction indicated. But they had not gone far when Kushtu noticed a little pool, fringed by rushes.

'Let us sit here, just for a little while,' she said,

hoping to postpone their departure.

'I'm sorry . . .' Amyas began and then stopped as a very odd noise broke the stillness.

'Whatever is it?' whispered Kushtu.

'I think it's . . . a . . . frog of some kind. Yes, there it is,' said Amyas, and pointed to a little frog scarcely distinguishable from the stone on which it sat on the far side of the pool.

The noise now increased in volume while, at the same time, the frog's cheeks billowed out on either side like two balloons.

'Look . . . oh look!' Kushtu cried, and could say no more as peal after peal of laughter drowned her words. It really was the most comical sight she had ever seen!

Amyas glanced from her to the frog and back to Kushtu, hardly daring to believe his eyes, as Kushtu's slender frame shook with laughter.

'Princess, you're laughing,' he cried. 'You've regained your sense of humour.'

'Well, he . . . he's so funny,' gasped Kushtu, blowing out her own cheeks in imitation of the frog, which made Amyas laugh too.

'What's so funny?' asked the frog hoarsely, interrupting his strange procedure.

'You . . . you are,' gasped Kushtu.

'I'm glad it amuses you.'

'Whyever do you do it?' asked Kushtu gently, sensing she had hurt the little creature's feelings.

'To try and attract a mate, as my voice is not very strong. So far I've had no success,' said the frog.

'But you've done something much more important. You've made the Princess laugh,' Amyas told him.

'So he did,' said Kushtu, and began laughing again at the mere recollection.

'Is she really a Princess?' asked the frog, awed.

'Of course she is. The Princess Kushtu,' replied Amyas.

'Oh! and I'm Plop. Shall I make her laugh again?' asked the frog and puffed out his cheeks once more. To such effect that both Amyas and Kushtu laughed again, even louder.

'It may amuse the Princess but it hasn't brought me a mate,' croaked the frog presently after looking around, in vain, for company. 'I'm so very lonely here.'

'Then why not come home with us? There are pools of all kinds in the royal grounds. You won't be lonely there,' said Kushtu.

'And be a royal frog?' asked the little creature.

'If that's what you want,' said Kushtu, smiling.

'Then I'll come with you,' replied Plop, and hopped into the pool to swim towards them.

'How shall we carry him?' asked Kushtu.

'Like this,' said Amyas, and pulled off his neckerchief, which he dabbled in the pool, before wrapping the frog within and slipping it into his pocket. 'Does that suit you, Plop?' he said.

'Admirably,' came the faint reply.

10

The Return

It was very soon after leaving the wood that they saw a party of horsemen in the distance.

'Who can they be, I wonder?' asked Kushtu, shielding her eyes with a hand.

'I hope they intend us no harm,' replied Amyas, recalling their meeting with Crukhid.

'Of course not,' cried Kushtu, who had just recognised the colours they bore. 'I can see the royal standard.'

It was indeed a search party that was one of several sent out by the King to look for his daughter.

'They must be looking for us,' Kushtu cried, and snatched off her cap to wave it vigorously which caused her hair to fall down over her shoulders.

'I'm afraid they are,' replied Amyas gloomily.

'Yes, here they come,' cried Kushtu, because

the file of horsemen were now seen to be heading towards them. 'And look, oh Amyas, do look, they have our two ponies.'

And there, sure enough, led by one of the troopers, were the two moorland ponies trotting along briskly. 'Now we shall be able to ride them home again,' she added joyously.

Her joy, however, was to be short-lived. The officer in charge, having first assured himself of her identity and despatching a messenger to acquaint the King of his daughter's safety, insisted she must travel in a litter which was quickly being lashed together.

'But why must I go in that?' asked Kushtu, when all her objections had proved to be in vain.

'Those are my orders, Princess,' replied the officer briefly, and would say no more.

It was one of the troopers, taking pity on the Princess, who answered her questions about how and when they had found the ponies. It seemed that a day or two after their foray into the desert in search of her, they had encountered Crukhid, and immediately recognised the ponies among the file of camels as belonging to the palace. When asked how they came to be in his

possession, Crukhid told them he had found the
ponies wandering in the desert, untended. He
voiced no objection when the troopers claimed
them and wisely made no mention of his meeting
with Amyas and the Princess.

By this time the litter was ready and Kushtu,
following Amyas's advice, allowed herself to be
placed within, but not before she had seen

Amyas mounted upon a horse, attached by a leading rein to one of the troopers.

And that was how they travelled to the city, where a closed carriage was waiting just within the gates. At a sign from its coachman, the officer brought his men to a halt, taking care that the litter stopped close by the carriage.

'You may descend now, Princess,' he said, and gave her his hand to help her alight. 'A carriage waits for you.'

The ride in the litter had been most uncomfortable and Kushtu was glad to exchange it for a carriage. 'But where is Amyas, where is my Protector?' she asked, while ascending the steps.

'You may well ask,' was the reply, from within the carriage, uttered in a voice which Kushtu knew very well.

'Why, Father, how very cross you sound,' said Kushtu, as she sat down upon the seat, facing the King. His crown had slipped to one side and he looked very angry.

'With good reason, daughter,' replied the King, while signalling the carriage to drive on.

'But where is Amyas? Why does he not ride with us?'

'Because the less you see of that young man the better.'

'But I've fallen in love with him,' she cried.

'Then you'll just have to fall out of love,' replied the King.

'Why should I?' asked Kushtu.

'Why? You dare to ask me why? After all the worry you've given your mother and me? Half my soldiery have been scouring the country and beyond, looking for you, I'll have you know.'

'There was no need,' said Kushtu sulkily. 'We came to no harm.'

'That may or may not be true,' replied the King.

'He took great care of me. And it was you who appointed him as my Protector,' said Kushtu.

'And a fine one he turned out to be. Luring you into the desert and who knows where besides?'

'Did Cousin Cassie tell you that? After giving us her promise not to say where we had gone?' asked Kushtu.

'And she kept her promise. All she would admit was that you had gone after some bird. And birds fly south at this time of year,' replied the King drily.

'And now that you have found us what do you intend?' asked Kushtu.

'We have not yet decided. Bread and water for you, I suspect.'

'And Amyas?'

'Banishment, at the very least,' replied the King, as the carriage came to an abrupt halt.

11

A Change of Heart

Although the King had given strict instructions that the carriage was to pull up in a secluded part of the palace grounds, so as not to attract any attention, a small crowd had gathered. There was the Queen, of course, together with a few of her ladies, Kushtu's old nurse, some courtiers, a stable-lad or two, and some of the house servants.

The King was the first to alight, followed immediately by his daughter, just as the party of troopers, with Amyas in their midst, was heard clattering over the cobbles.

'Are my orders never to be obeyed?' growled the King to the Queen while surveying the onlookers with a frown. 'I thought I told you, wife, that there was to be no fuss?'

'I did my best, but everyone was so overjoyed at hearing the Princess was safe and on her way home,' replied the Queen, and went to embrace her daughter, much to the King's annoyance.

'In that case they will be able to see how we deal with charlatans,' replied the King and, raising his voice, 'Bring Amyas to me,' he roared.

The onlookers all craned their necks, pushing and jostling, in the hope of seeing the young man who stepped out from among the troopers to approach the King.

'Ah! Amyas, there you are,' cried Kushtu, and would have gone to him had the King not restrained her.

'Control yourself, daughter,' he muttered. 'Remember who you are.'

'Don't be too hard on him, husband,' whispered the Queen, looking at Amyas standing there, so brave and steadfast.

'I think I owe you an explanation, Your Majesty,' Amyas said.

'You owe us more than that,' growled the King. 'You may regard yourself as fortunate, young man, not to be thrown into the dungeons. Instead, you will leave this land immediately, never to return.'

'But, Sire . . .' Amyas began.

'Immediately!' repeated the King while the Princess reached out her arms and whispered brokenly, 'Father, I beg you . . . please listen . . .' and the Queen added her entreaty, 'Dear husband, pray consider . . . At least give him time to prepare . . .'

'He came here with little – he shall leave here with less,' replied the King sternly.

Amyas's face had gone very pale at hearing he was to be banished. Nevertheless he was able to speak out firmly. 'Then if that is your will, Sire, I must first return this to the Princess,' he said, withdrawing a damp bundle from within his pocket.

Gently he parted the kerchief to disclose the little frog which stared about him, unblinkingly, for a moment or two. Then, in one gigantic leap, he launched himelf into the air to land right on top of the King's bald head. Maybe he mistook that shiny pate for a pool of water, or maybe he just wanted to surprise the King. He certainly succeeded, because the King gave a loud gasp as he clutched at his crown, to prevent it from falling to the ground, while his face mottled with anger to hear the amusement of the crowd. It

quickly cleared, though, when he saw his daughter laughing, laughing uncontrollably, at the
absurd spectacle he presented.

'Why . . . why . . . was I not told you had
found your sense of humour?' he asked, even as
his daughter removed Plop from her father's
head to point the frog in the direction of the
nearest pool.

'I thought you knew,' she said.

'How could I? This is the only time I've seen you laugh.'

'There was so little to laugh about,' she replied meekly.

'I think you owe Amyas an apology, husband. He seems to have succeeded where all else has failed,' said the Queen.

'Indeed I do, but not here,' replied the King and, turning to Amyas, 'Come, lad, let us all withdraw. You shall tell us, the two of you, all that happened since you left us – and, more importantly, exactly how Kushtu found her sense of humour.'

And so it was in the seclusion of the King's room, where refreshments were hurriedly sent for, that the King and Queen heard all about those adventures in the desert. The account was frequently interrupted by the Princess's laughter as she recalled some of those adventures. This so entranced the King that he readily agreed to Kushtu's request that she be allowed to marry Amyas. Indeed, the King was so happy at the change in his daughter that, to the great delight of the Queen, he even named the wedding day.

Thus, all was bustle and excitement in the

palace during the coming weeks. It began in the kitchens, and overflowed into the Court Dressmaker's, as preparations went ahead for the wedding. The list of invitations was truly enormous and heading that list was – yes, you've guessed – the name of Cousin Cassie.

It also included the little armadillo, Tampala the elephant and of course, Plop. Whether or not those invitations ever reached them, or whether they came to the wedding, I cannot tell you, as none of them ever remained in one place for very long. What I can tell you is that the wedding was a very grand affair which is much talked about even to this day!